Great Job!

Achievement Award

_____

(name)

has completed

Pre-K

School Games

on

_____

(date)

Hurray!   **Well done!**

Congratulations!

Alphabet

Practice writing the uppercase letter and complete the word.
Then, practice writing the lowercase letter and complete the word.

A A A

_pple

a a

_nt

B B

_ear

b b

_all

Practice writing the uppercase letter and complete the word.
Then, practice writing the lowercase letter and complete the word.

_up

_ake

_od

_rum

Alphabet

Practice writing the uppercase letter and complete the word.
Then, practice writing the lowercase letter and complete the word.

Eagle

earth

Frog

ish

Alphabet

Practice writing the uppercase letter and complete the word.
Then, practice writing the lowercase letter and complete the word.

G g

__ift

g

__oose

H h

__en

h

__at

Alphabet

Practice writing the uppercase letter and complete the word.
Then, practice writing the lowercase letter and complete the word.

I

i

_sland

_groo

_am

_ug

Practice writing the uppercase letter and complete the word.
Then, practice writing the lowercase letter and complete the word.

_ite

_ing

_eaf

_og

Alphabet

Practice writing the uppercase letter and complete the word.
Then, practice writing the lowercase letter and complete the word.

_uffin

_oon

_est

_et

Alphabet

Practice writing the uppercase letter and complete the word.
Then, practice writing the lowercase letter and complete the word.

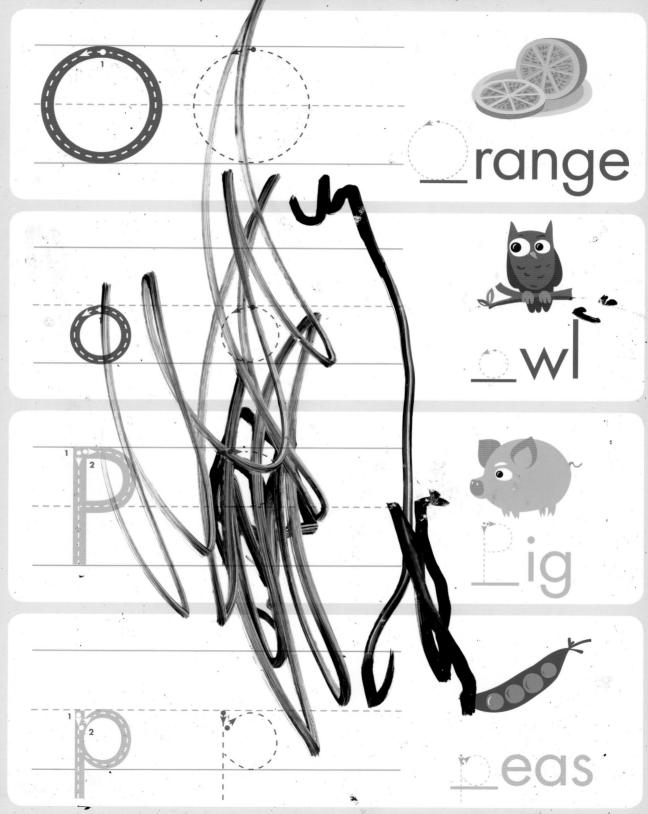

_range

_wl

_ig

_eas

Alphabet

Practice writing the uppercase letter and complete the word.
Then, practice writing the lowercase letter and complete the word.

Queen

quail

Ring

rabbit

Alphabet

Practice writing the uppercase letter and complete the word.
Then, practice writing the lowercase letter and complete the word.

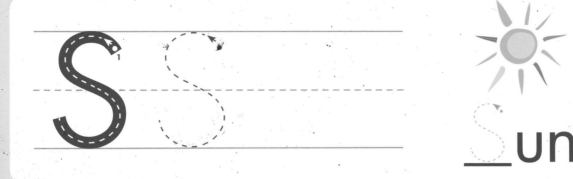

__un

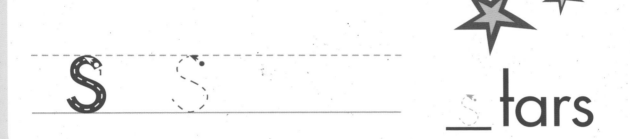

__tars

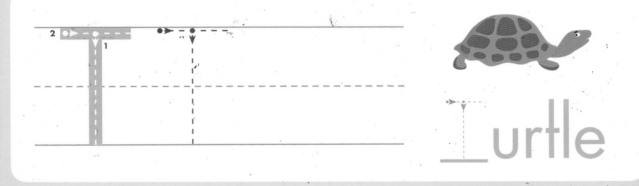

__urtle

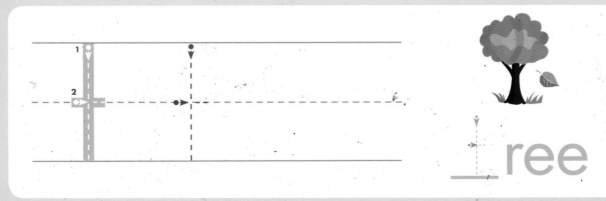

__ree

Alphabet

Practice writing the uppercase letter and complete the word.
Then, practice writing the lowercase letter and complete the word.

U U

_rchin

U U

_nicorn

V V

_iolin

V V

_ase

Alphabet

Practice writing the uppercase letter and complete the word.
Then, practice writing the lowercase letter and complete the word.

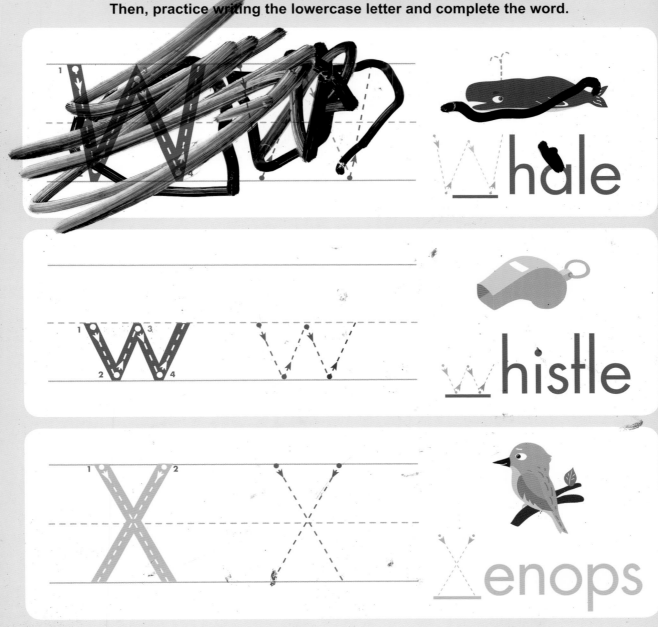

__hale

W w __histle

X x __enops

X x fo__

Alphabet

Practice writing the uppercase letter and complete the word.
Then, practice writing the lowercase letter and complete the word.

__am

__arn

__ebra

__ipper

Trace the numbers and count the objects. Then, circle every like number you see.

Trace the numbers and count the objects. Then, circle every like number you see.

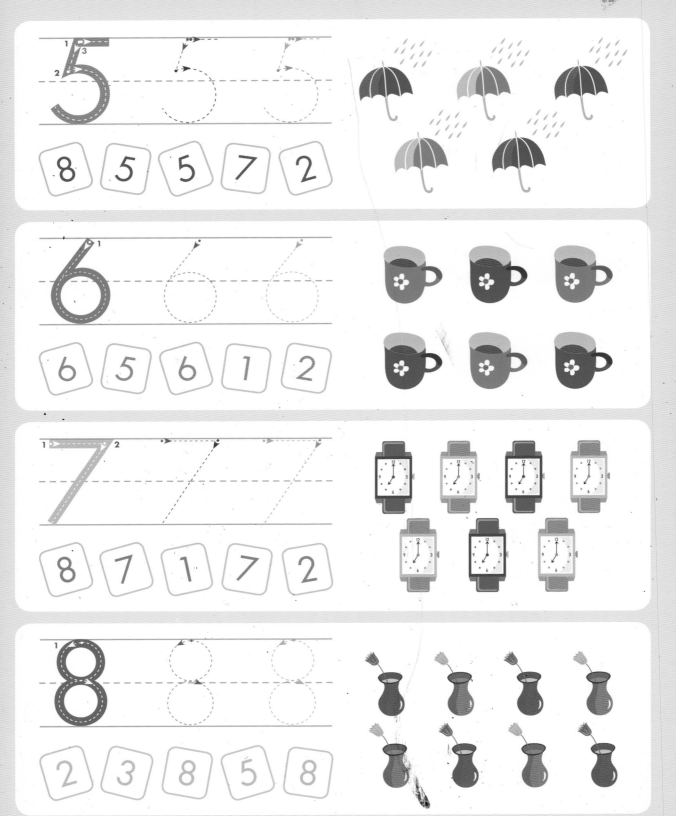

Numbers

Trace the numbers and count the objects. Then, circle every like number you see.

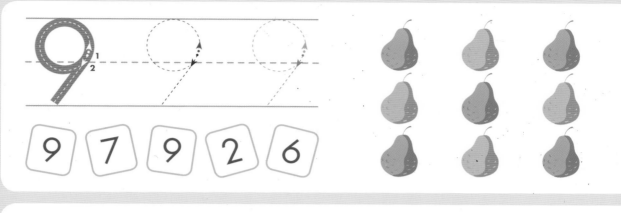

9   7   9   2   6

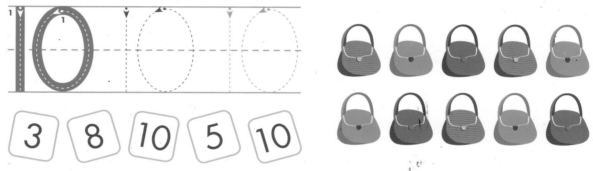

3   8   10   5   10

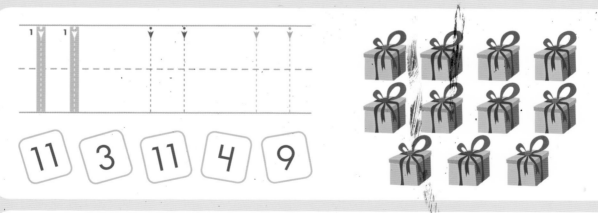

11   3   11   4   9

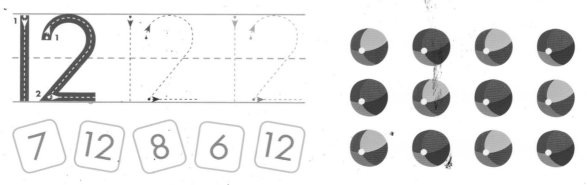

7   12   8   6   12

Colors

Read the name of each color aloud. Then, circle all of the objects that match.

Red

Orange

Yellow

Green

Colors

Read the name of each color aloud. Then, circle all of the objects that match.

Blue

Purple

Teal

Pink

Colors

Read the name of each color aloud. Then, circle all of the objects that match.

Brown

Gray

Black

White

Colors

Draw a line to match the things that are the same color.

Shapes

Trace all the shapes you see that have a dashed line.

Circles

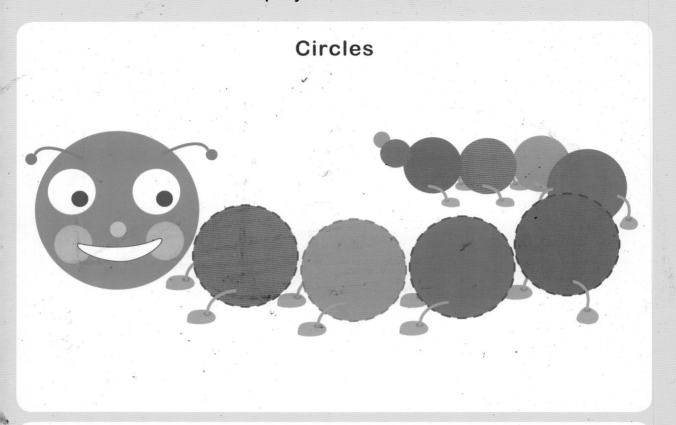

Ovals

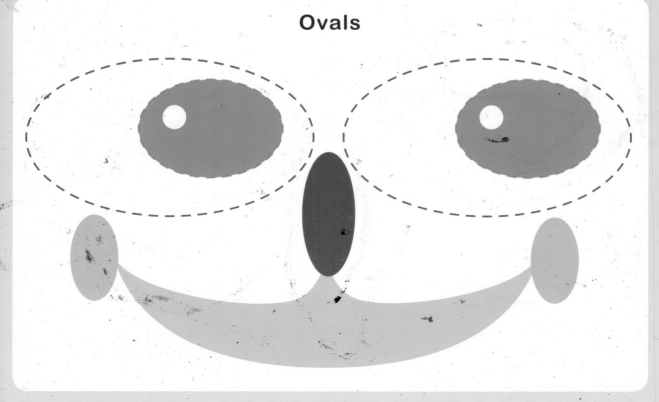

Shapes

Trace all the shapes you see that have a dashed line.

Squares

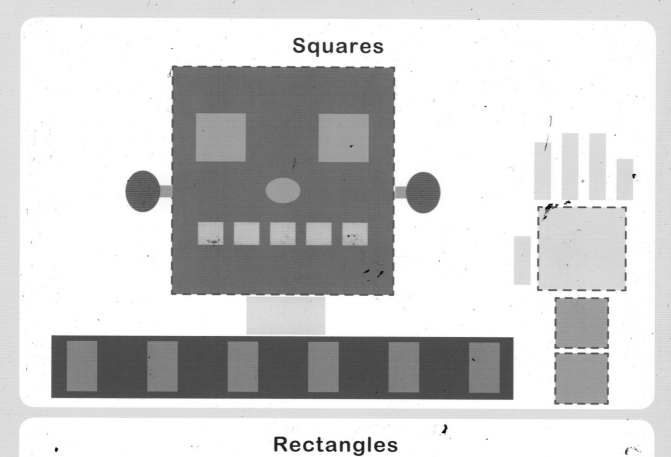

Rectangles

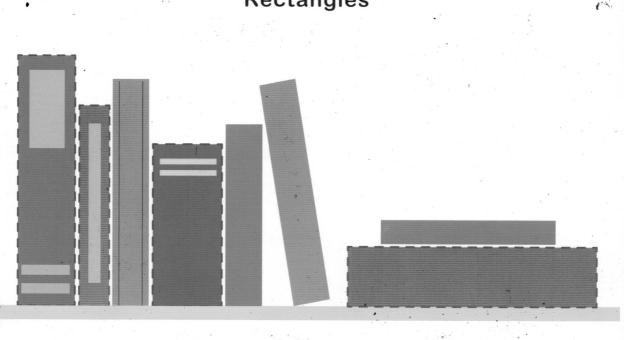

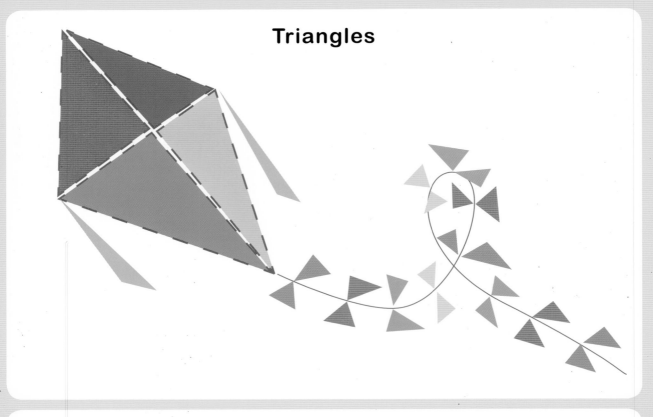

Shapes

Trace all the shapes you see that have a dashed line.

Triangles

Diamonds

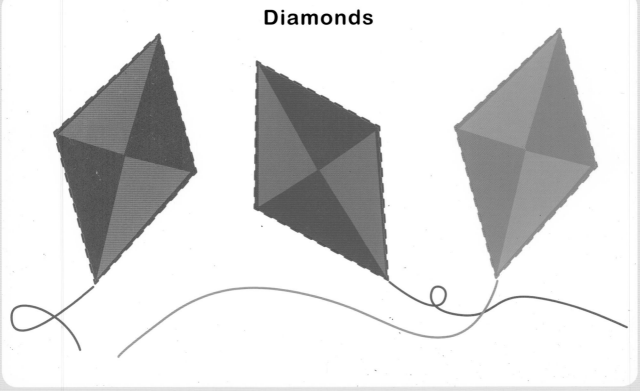

Shapes

Trace all the shapes you see that have a dashed line.

Stars

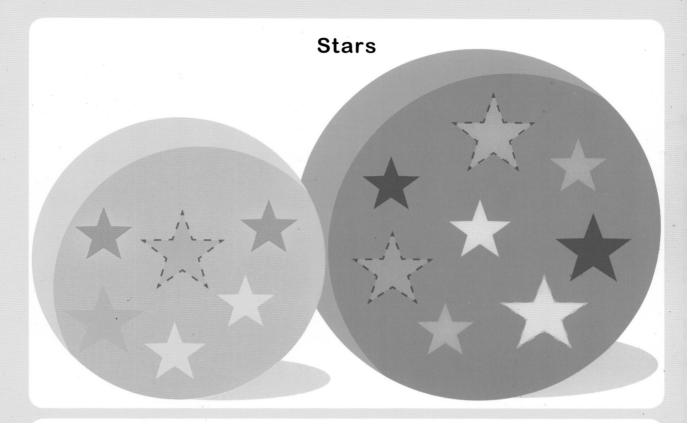

Hearts

Shapes

Circle all of the objects you see that match the title shape.

Finding Circles!

Finding Ovals!

Circle all of the objects you see that match the title shape:

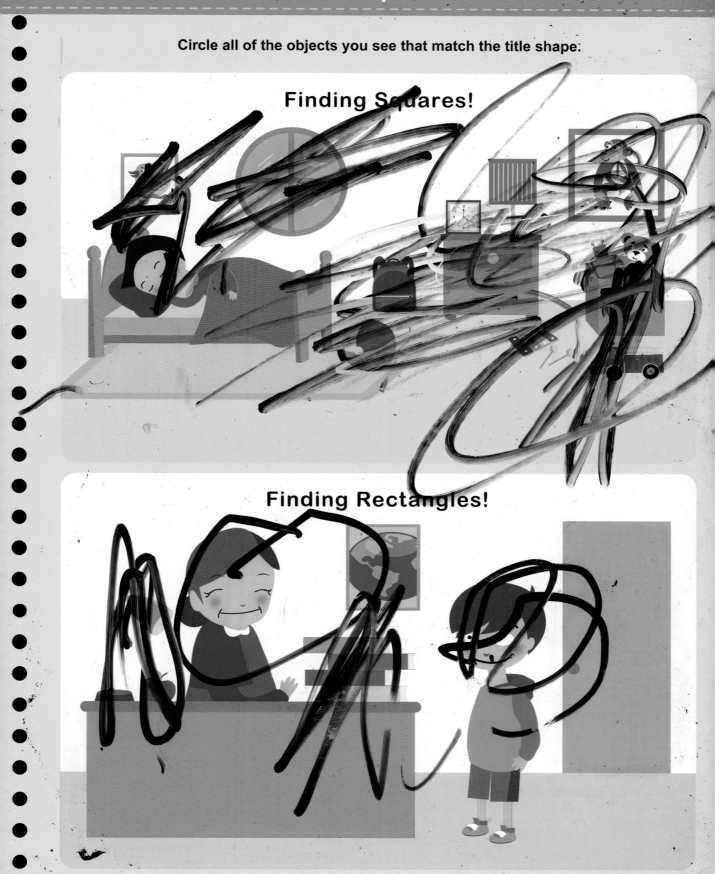

Finding Squares!

Finding Rectangles!

Shapes

Circle all of the objects you see that match the title shape.

Finding Triangles!

Finding Diamonds!

Shapes

Circle all of the objects you see that match the title shape.

Finding Stars!

Finding Hearts!

Opposites

Follow the instructions below.

Fast or Slow:
Circle the animals that are fast.
Cross out the things that are slow.

Open or Closed:
Circle the things that are open.
Cross out the things that are closed.

Tall or Short:
Circle the things that are tall.
Cross out the things that are short.

Big or Little:
Circle the things that are big.
Cross out the things that are little.

Opposites

Follow the instructions below.

Hot or Cold:
Circle the things that are hot.
Cross out the things that are cold.

Full or Empty:
Circle the things that are full.
Cross out the things that are empty.

Soft or Hard:
Circle the things that are soft.
Cross out the things that are hard.

On or Off:
Circle the things that are on.
Cross out the things that are off.

Sorting

Circle the items that belong.

Up in the Sky

Underwater

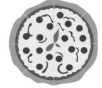

At the Market

In the Forest

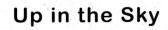

Sorting

Circle the items that belong.

On the Farm

At School

At the Beach

In Outer Space

Sorting

Draw a line to match the things that go together.

Practice saying the vowels and consonants aloud.
Then, circle all the things whose name makes the title sound.

Vowels

Consonants

A Sound

B Sound

Phonics

Circle all the things whose name makes the title sound.

C Sound

D Sound

E Sound

F Sound

Phonics

Circle all the things whose name makes the title sound.

G Sound

H Sound

I Sound

J Sound

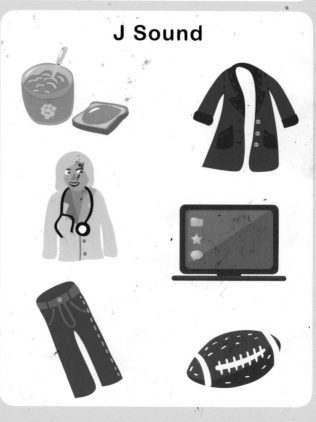

Phonics

Circle all the things whose name makes the title sound.

K Sound

L Sound

M Sound

N Sound

Phonics

Circle all the things whose name makes the title sound.

O Sound

P Sound

Q Sound

R Sound

Phonics

Circle all the things whose name makes the title sound.

S Sound

T Sound

U Sound

V Sound

Phonics

Circle all the things whose name makes the title sound.

W Sound

X Sound

Y Sound

Z Sound

Counting

Count the things below. Then, draw a line to match the correct number.

Plates

Pillows

Marbles

Buttons

Plates: 6, 2, 4

Pillows: 5, 1, 3

Marbles: 12, 7, 10

Buttons: 12, 10, 11

Counting

Count the number of things. Then, write the correct number in the box next to it.

Hats

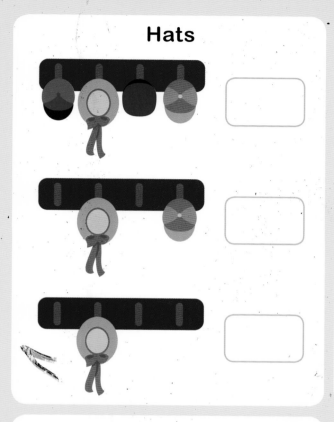

Windows

Keys

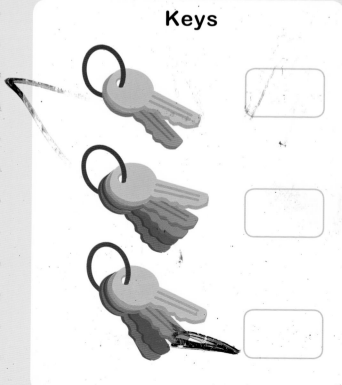

Candles

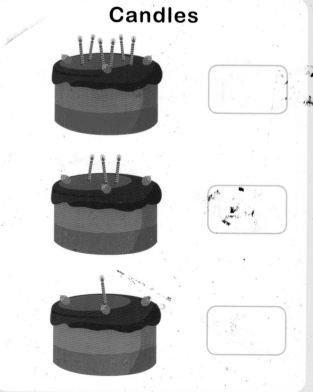

Sight Words

Trace and write the sight word. Then, see how it is used in the sentences.

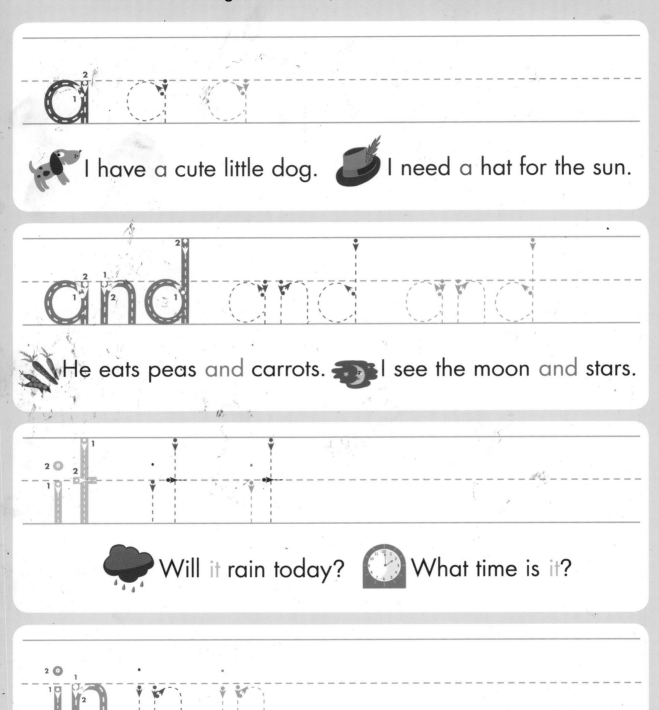

a a a

I have a cute little dog.   I need a hat for the sun.

and and and

He eats peas and carrots.   I see the moon and stars.

it it it

Will it rain today?   What time is it?

in in in

 The mitt is in the yard.   We are in the car.

Sight Words

Trace and write the sight word. Then, see how it is used in the sentences.

run run run

 You can run very quickly. Can I run up the hill?

see see see

 I see a rainbow. They see a bus.

can can can

 They can dance. We can play.

find find find

 We find crayons. They find milk.

Rhyming

Say each word aloud. Then draw lines to match the words that sound alike.

 CAR

 BEE

 BAT

 CAKE

 SNAKE

 HAT

 TREE

 JAR

 PIE

 BED

 VEST

 DUCK

 RED

 NEST

 TRUCK

 TIE

 DOG

 SKATE

 BELL

 SLIDE

 BRIDE

 SHELL

 GATE

 FROG

 WHALE

 KING

 BLUE

 SPOON

 SWING

 SNAIL

 MOON

 GLUE

Rhyming

Say each word aloud. Then draw lines to match the words that sound alike.

 HAND

 CLOCK

 GREEN

 SAND

 SOCK

 BEAN

 DOOR

 FOUR

 CHAIR

 BUG

 BROWN

 RAIN

 TRAIN

 CLOWN

 RUG

 SQUARE

 GOAT

 CONE

 PLATE

 HOUSE

 BONE

 BOAT

 MOUSE

 EIGHT

 KITE

 TEN

 FAN

 LIGHT

 BREAD

 CAN

 PEN

 SLED

Science

Circle all the living things you see.

Plants

Animals

Cross out all the non-living things you see.

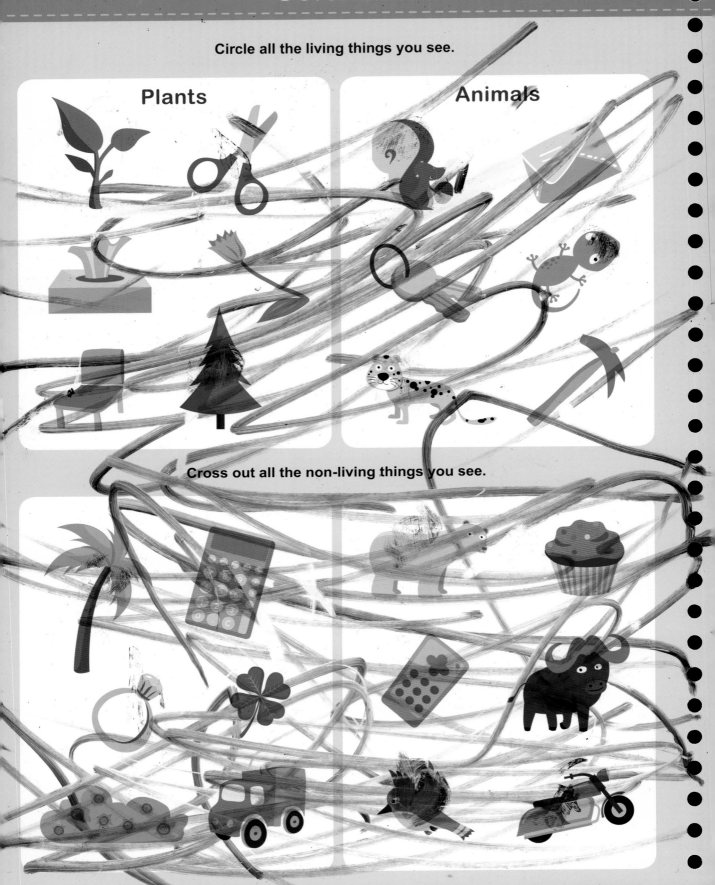

Draw a line to match each baby animal to its parent.

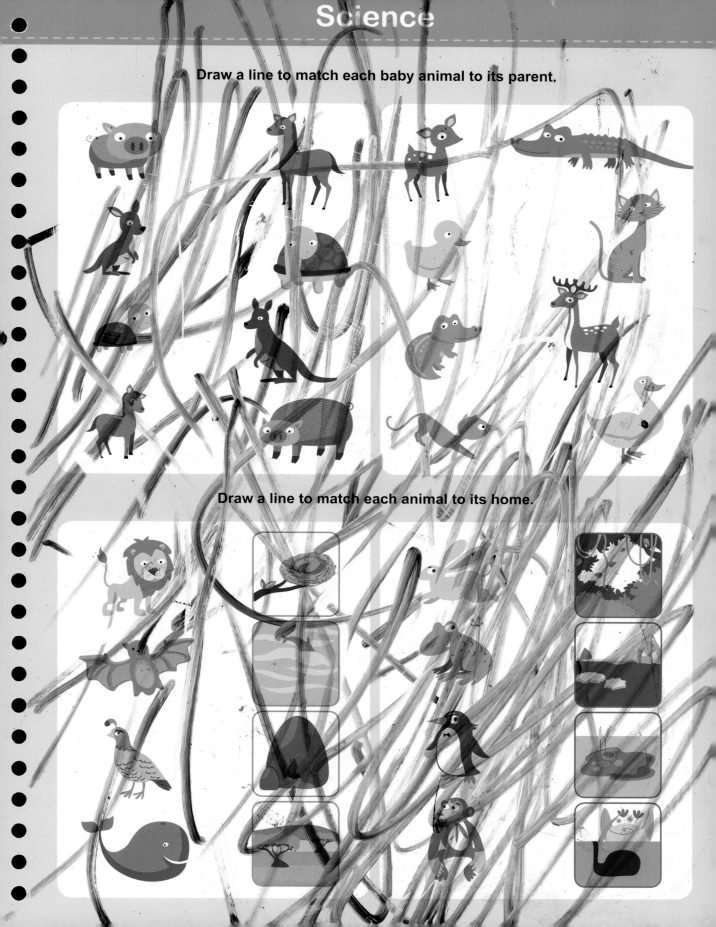

Draw a line to match each animal to its home.

Science

Circle all the things that need electricity.
Cross out all the things that don't need electricity.

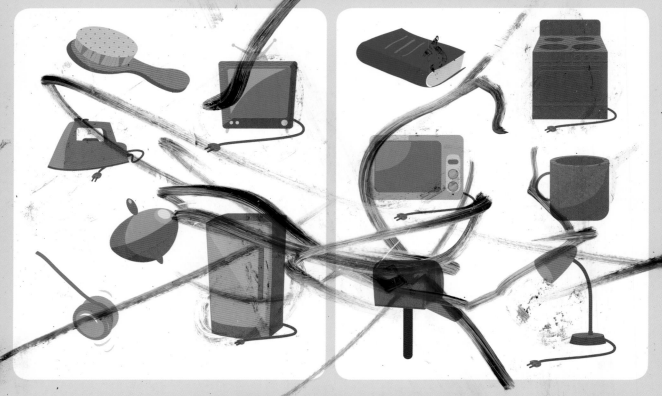

Circle all the things you see that are ...

Hot!

Cold!

CONTROLLING
YOUR
FAT TOOTH

OTHER BOOKS BY JOSEPH C. PISCATELLA

DON'T EAT YOUR HEART OUT COOKBOOK
CHOICES FOR A HEALTHY HEART

CONTROLLING
=YOUR=
FAT TOOTH

BY JOSEPH C. PISCATELLA
RECIPES BY BERNIE PISCATELLA

WORKMAN PUBLISHING, NEW YORK

ACKNOWLEDGMENTS

This book has become a reality thanks to the support and cooperation of many people. In particular, we are grateful to the medical professionals who gave of their time and expertise, providing valuable appraisals of and suggestions concerning the manuscript. These include Adam Drewnowski, Ph.D., Evette Hackman, Ph.D., R.D., Barry Franklin, Ph.D., and Mary Prather, R.D. In addition, we'd like to thank Sally Barline and Patty Brustkern for their recipe suggestions and endless hours of proofreading; Julie Headrick for her tireless hours of nutritional analysis; Betty Kirk, Peggy Paradise and Trina Rubel for their encouragement and recipe suggestions; Anne Piscatella, Joey Piscatella and Brent Knittel for their eagerness and good humor as chief recipe testers. And finally, our thanks to Peter Workman for his faith in our project, to Sally Kovalchick for being the magnificent editor that she's always been, and to Lynn Strong for her fine manuscript work.

Copyright © 1991 by Joseph C. Piscatella

Library of Congress Cataloging-in-Publication Data
Piscatella, Joseph C.
    Controlling your fat tooth/by Joseph C. Piscatella.
    p. cm.
  Includes index.
  ISBN 0-89480-431-6
    1. Low-cholesterol diet. 2. Low-cholesterol diet—Recipes.
I. Title.
RM237.75.P57 1990   90-50361
613.2′8—dc20   CIP

Cover Design by Lisa Hollander

Workman Publishing Company, Inc.
708 Broadway
New York, New York 10003

First printing April 1991
Manufactured in the United States

10 9 8 7 6 5 4 3 2 1